I0814805

ORCA FOOTPRINTS

Our Plastic Problem

A CALL FOR GLOBAL SOLUTIONS

MEGAN DURNFORD

ORCA BOOK PUBLISHERS

For everyone who helps to protect the natural world.

Published in Canada and the United States in 2025 by Orca Book Publishers.
orcabook.com

Library and Archives Canada Cataloguing in Publication
Title: Our plastic problem : a call for global solutions / Megan Durnford.
Names: Durnford, Megan, author.
Series: Orca footprints ; 33.
Description: Series statement: Orca footprints ; 33 | Includes bibliographical references and index.
Identifiers: Canadiana (print) 20240320042 | Canadiana (ebook) 20240320077 |
ISBN 9781459836709 (hardcover) | ISBN 9781459836716 (PDF) | ISBN 9781459836723 (EPUB)
Subjects: LCSH: Plastics—Juvenile literature. | LCSH: Plastics—Environmental aspects—Juvenile literature. |
LCSH: Plastic scrap—Environmental aspects—Juvenile literature. |
LCSH: Environmental protection—Citizen participation—Juvenile literature.
Classification: LCC TD798 .D87 2025 | DDC j363.72/88—dc23

Library of Congress Control Number: 2024933314

Summary: Part of the nonfiction Orca Footprints series, this book explores the history and uses of plastic and the resulting environmental problems. Illustrated with photographs throughout.

Orca Book Publishers is committed to reducing the consumption of nonrenewable resources in the production of our books. We make every effort to use materials that support a sustainable future.

Orca Book Publishers gratefully acknowledges the support for its publishing programs provided by the following agencies: the Government of Canada, the Canada Council for the Arts and the Province of British Columbia through the BC Arts Council and the Book Publishing Tax Credit.

Front cover photos by Ron Levine/Getty Images and SolStock/Getty Images.
Design by Dahlia Yuen.
Edited by Kirstie Hudson.

Printed and bound in South Korea.

28 27 26 25 • 1 2 3 4

We can all help to prevent plastic pollution.
FG TRADE LATIN/GETTY IMAGES

Contents

CHAPTER ONE
MIRACLE MATERIAL

CHAPTER TWO
PLASTIC FOREVER

CHAPTER THREE
GLOBAL PROBLEMS NEED GLOBAL SOLUTIONS

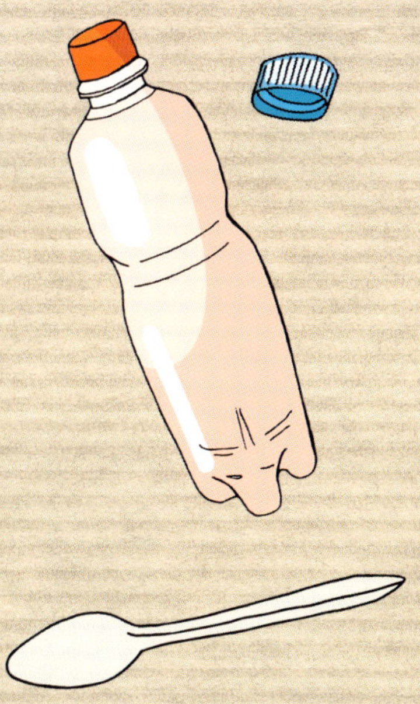

CHAPTER FOUR
BEYOND PLASTIC

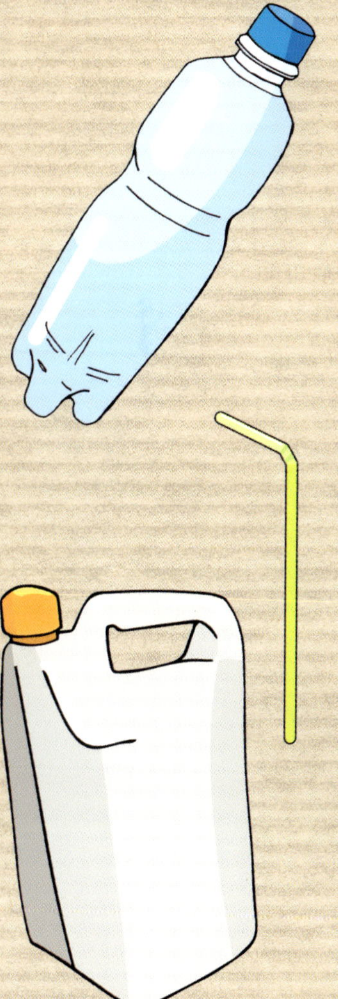

Introduction

When I travel, I always bring a snack-filled reusable metal container and my reusable bamboo cutlery set.
HUGH DURNFORD-DIONNE

When I was growing up in the 1960s, plastic was considered a miraculous material. Plastic made life easy. Why would you wash, dry and iron a fabric tablecloth when you could simply wipe a plastic tablecloth clean? In fact, this ultramodern material was so exciting that most mothers (and yes, it was mostly women in those days) in our neighborhood regularly hosted and attended sales parties for plastic food containers. Now, several decades later, the word *plastic* is more likely to be associated with pollution and harmful health effects than parties. What happened?

The story of plastic is complicated because there are so many different kinds of plastic and because we are all completely dependent on plastic from the moment we wake up to the moment we go to sleep. (Not to mention the plastic present in the mattresses we sleep on!) Plastic serves a lot of important

Tupperware parties were popular in the 1950s and '60s. Neighbors and friends would gather to purchase new plastic containers from a salesperson—and also to catch up on one another's news.
STATE LIBRARY AND ARCHIVES OF FLORIDA/WIKIMEDIA COMMONS/PUBLIC DOMAIN

purposes in our society. Plastic keeps food fresh. It helps protect us from contagious diseases in the hospital. It is light, flexible, strong, convenient—and inexpensive. But plastic has been a victim of its own success. It is so incredibly useful that in the last 60 years, the world has produced more than 8 billion tons (7.25 billion metric tons) of plastic. And, believe it or not, all of that plastic is still hanging around in one form or another. Join me for a journey through our plastic world to explore the good, the bad and the big questions about this remarkable substance.

ISABEL PAVIA/GETTY IMAGES

CHAPTER ONE

Miracle Material

Everything our early human ancestors needed to survive was made out of natural materials such as wood and leather because those were the only materials they had. But today a vast collection of different synthetic materials has profoundly changed every aspect of modern daily life.

A long time ago, billiard balls were made of ivory from elephant tusks. The invention of celluloid was great news for elephants!

(MAIN) CHUCHART DUANGDAW/GETTY IMAGES; (INSET) DIVISION OF MEDICINE AND SCIENCE, NATIONAL MUSEUM OF AMERICAN HISTORY, SMITHSONIAN INSTITUTION

SAVING ELEPHANTS

In the 19th century, ivory from elephant tusks was used for making household objects like combs, piano keys and the balls used to play a game called ***billiards***. As billiards became increasingly popular, some people worried that the game might cause elephants to go extinct. When John Wesley Hyatt heard this terrible news, he decided to create a substance to replace ivory. Hyatt had never studied chemistry at school, but he really liked to invent things. He figured he could come up with something useful. Hyatt also wanted to win some money. He had heard that a company in New York was offering $10,000 in gold to whoever could successfully create a substitute for ivory.

Plastic is fantastic. It can be turned into almost anything!
CURTOICURTO/GETTY IMAGES

After several years experimenting with a lot of different (and dangerous and explosive!) substances, Hyatt did invent a substitute for ivory. Then Hyatt's brother, Isaiah, came up with a name for this new substance. He called it *celluloid* because it reminded him of ***cellulose***. Celluloid was the first useful synthetic plastic.

In the late 1930s, the inventors of a new synthetic fiber considered more than 350 possible names—including novasilk, silmon, amidarn and tensheer—before choosing the word *nylon*.

FROM COMBS TO CINEMA

Celluloid was an amazing substance. It could be molded into all kinds of different shapes, and it could also be hardened. Ultimately it was not very useful for making billiard balls, because it didn't bounce like ivory. But it turned out to be an ideal material for combs. Celluloid combs did not deteriorate when they got wet, they were available in a huge range of colors and patterns, and they were affordable. Real tortoiseshell combs were very expensive. Celluloid combs colored to look like tortoiseshell were not. Celluloid was also useful for making toothbrush handles, false teeth and detachable shirt collars.

NATIONAL MUSEUM OF AMERICAN HISTORY/CC0

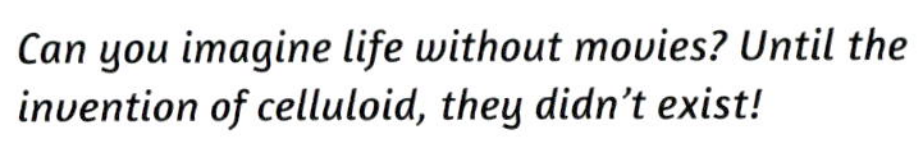

Can you imagine life without movies? Until the invention of celluloid, they didn't exist!
BELLA FALK/ALAMY STOCK PHOTO

One of the most exciting new uses of celluloid was for storing images. This was the beginning of a new era for photography. Guess what happened next? The Lumière brothers in France invented cinema. They had a feeling that "moving pictures" on celluloid film projected in a theater might be really popular. They were right! Celluloid led to a brand-new form of entertainment.

Nylon parachutes are lightweight and very strong. During World War II, these parachutes helped thousands of paratroopers land safely on the ground.
JOHNCAIRNS/GETTY IMAGES

PLASTIC GOES TO WAR

In the United States, plastic production tripled during World War II. The military effort depended on plastic for many different things, including nylon for making parachutes, ropes, helmet liners and goggles. Acrylic plastic sheets were used to make aircraft windows, and plastic wrap protected military equipment during shipping. After the war ended, plastic manufacturers quickly switched their focus to consumer items.

WHAT IS PLASTIC?

There are thousands of different types of plastics, with a range of characteristics. Some are thin and delicate, some are very stretchy, and some are strong enough to use for building bridges. What they have in common is that they all come from ***fossil fuels*** and they are all composed of ***polymers***.

RAIMUND KOCH/GETTY IMAGES

The first plastic Christmas tree, introduced in 1957, had a brown polystyrene trunk and green polyethylene branches.

HOW IS PLASTIC MADE?

Plastic is made in huge ***petrochemical plants***. There is a different recipe for each ***resin***. Polyethylene, one of the most popular plastics for making packaging, is used to make white plastic grocery bags. Here's how it is made. First ethane is sent to a special furnace called a *cracker*, where it is mixed with steam and flash-heated to over 1472°F (800°C). As the ***ethane*** is "cracked" (the ***molecular bonds*** of ethane are broken), it is transformed into ethylene gas. The ethylene is repeatedly heated and cooled under high pressure. A few other chemicals, such as butane and propylene, are added in until polyethylene is formed. Liquid polyethylene is cooled and then molded into long strings, which are cut into pellets called ***nurdles***. The pellets are shipped by railcar and boat to factories that make polyethylene products. It takes about 174 nurdles to make a plastic grocery bag.

Newly made plastic looks like spaghetti strands. After the strands harden, they are cut up into little pellets.

(TOP) CHELMICKY/GETTY IMAGES; (BOTTOM) HEMANTPHOTOGRAPHER/GETTY IMAGES

HUGH DURNFORD-DIONNE

Plastic Overload

Plastic is all around you. Have you ever tried counting all the different types of plastic things you use every day? Some are obvious, like a plastic cup. But you use hundreds of things made with plastic that are not so obvious. Did you know that the following things are made with plastic? Paper bills, pencils, balloons, glitter, contact lenses, jogging pants, electrical cords, nonstick pans, packing peanuts, pantyhose, ribbon, wallpaper, Scotch tape, stickers, Velcro, yoga mats, umbrellas and toothbrushes.

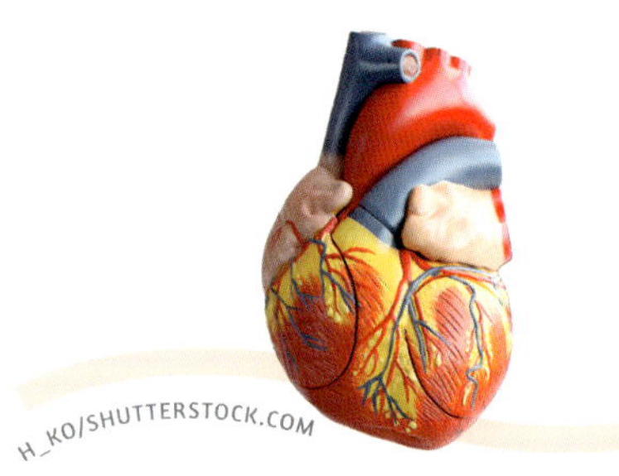

H_KO/SHUTTERSTOCK.COM

Plastic is commonly used to replace body parts. After surgeon William DeVries implanted the first permanent artificial heart in 1982, he famously said it snapped into place "just like closing Tupperware."

CAN PLASTIC SAVE YOUR LIFE?

Plastic has made a lot of modern medical miracles possible. Plastic pacemakers keep some people's hearts beating, plastic replacement joints keep people moving, and plastic veins keep blood flowing. Also, modern hospitals rely on easy-to-clean plastic surfaces and single-use disposable plastic items, such as syringes and gloves, to reduce the spread of ***microbes***.

At the beginning of the 20th century, metal, ceramics and glass were used for making medical equipment and storing medicine. These natural materials are very strong, and they can be sterilized, but they are not flexible, so there are limitations to how they can be used. As new plastics were invented, modern medicine found many uses for them. In the 1940s American blood banks used rubber tubing and glass bottles with rubber plugs to collect and store blood. This process was better than nothing, but sometimes during blood transfers, red blood cells were damaged. Also, bacteria and air bubbles sometimes contaminated the collected blood.

An innovative American surgeon named Carl Walter began to search for alternatives. One of the materials that caught his eye was ***PVC*** plastic treated with ***phthalates***. Walter began to experiment with containers and tubing made from this soft, flexible material. Plastic definitely made blood collection and storage easier. Now flexible plastic bags for delivering medications and nutrition through a tube are used in hospitals around the world.

Do you know anybody who was born prematurely, before their body was able to function independently? In the past, most "preemie" babies died shortly after birth. Since the creation of special neonatal units in the mid-1960s, preemie babies have been able to complete their development outside the womb. Preemie babies are completely dependent on the extremely thin plastic tubing that delivers food and medicine to their fragile bodies and the plastic tubing used to monitor their health.

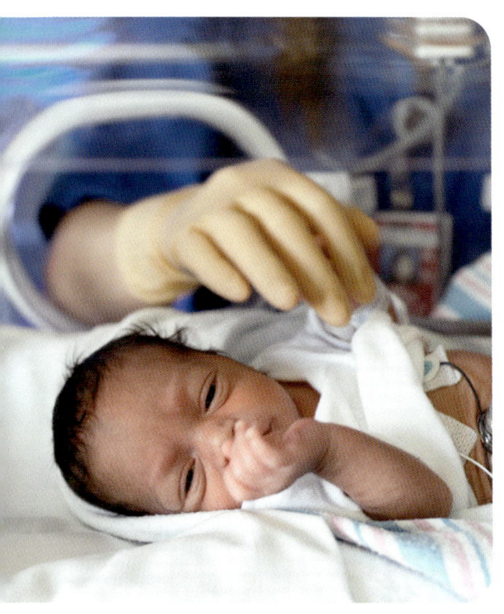

Plastic medical equipment helps premature babies (babies born before their bodies are fully developed) stay alive.

ER PRODUCTIONS LIMITED/GETTY IMAGES

Synthetic fabrics play an important role in our modern economy.

MEHTAP ORGUN/GETTY IMAGES

WEARING PLASTIC

Did you know that you wear plastic? If you have a bathing suit, a raincoat, rain boots, a windbreaker, jogging pants or any other clothing made from synthetic fibers, you are wearing materials made from plastic. Synthetic fabrics such as nylon, polyester and spandex don't need to be ironed and are flexible, easy to clean, waterproof—and cheap! So it is not surprising that nylon stockings have replaced silk stockings, vinyl raincoats have replaced the Macintosh (a coat made from rubber-coated cloth) and nylon bathing suits have replaced wool swimwear. The new synthetic materials were (and still are!) a great source of inspiration for fashion designers.

In the early 1980s, the textile industry in the northeastern United States was in steep decline. But the descendant of one old textile family took a chance on developing a new high-tech polyester product. The result, polar fleece, was kind of like sheepskin—except that it was warmer and cheaper than this natural material. A few years later another textile manufacturer started to make fleece from discarded plastic bottles. By turning plastic waste into valuable clothing, synthetic fleece *seemed* to be the most environmentally friendly fabric. In chapter 2, you will learn about the downside of this material.

Do you have a fleece hat too? Synthetic fabrics can be very cozy, and they dry fast.

CHIZUKO KOBAYASHI/GETTY IMAGES

PLASTIC AT PLAY

In 1967, New York City residents were asked to put their garbage in plastic bags rather than metal cans.

For most of human history, children have played with homemade toys made from cloth, wood, clay and other natural materials. The invention of plastic changed toys forever. After all, plastic can come in hundreds of forms, and remember, it's durable and cheap! Thanks to plastic, dolls can have soft, smooth skin. And their cute chubby plastic faces look more like real babies than those of the old-fashioned rag or ceramic dolls. Plastic's amazing versatility led to all kinds of new toys too.

In the late 1950s, American toy manufacturer Wham-O heard that bamboo hoops were extremely popular in Australia. Aussie teens loved the challenge of keeping hoops circling around their bodies by continuously shifting their hips so the hoops never fell to the floor. So Wham-O began to make plastic hoops from a new semirigid type of polyethylene in a range of colors. This new invention, called a Hula-Hoop, was wildly popular with American teens. Wham-O could barely keep up with demand. At its peak, it was transforming over a million pounds (more than 453,000 kilograms) of polyethylene a day into Hula-Hoops.

Throwaway Living

In the 1950s and '60s, the switch from natural materials to plastic was not just a switch to a new material. Ultimately it led to a new way of thinking about consumer products—making them disposable. At first North Americans did not want to buy disposable products, because they had learned during the long, difficult years of the Great Depression and World War II how to avoid waste. Their instinct was to reuse and repair everything, not toss things out.

But eventually marketers helped "reeducate" consumers to adapt to the age of "throwaway living." Consumers were taught to see the positive side of disposable plastics. These new products let people spend less time on boring tasks and have more time for enjoyable activities. Why wash dishes when you can just throw them out? Soon North Americans were happy to buy disposable versions of just about anything—disposable cameras, sandals, lighters, watches and decorations. Today many North American families are trying to move in the opposite direction.

PICS FIVE/SHUTTERSTOCK.COM

Plastic can be turned into almost anything. Most toys are made from this versatile material.

(LEFT) OLGA PANKOVA/GETTY IMAGES; (RIGHT) JARABEE123/GETTY IMAGES

TOY STORIES

You have probably played with a plastic Frisbee. Do you know the story behind this toy? Believe it or not, the original flying toy was a metal pie tin. William Frisbie ran a pie company in a small town near Yale University in Connecticut. When the Yale students took time off from studying, they would toss their empty Frisbie pie tins across the campus. Walter Frederick Morrison, an inventor from California, found ways to make flying discs faster and more stable. Wham-O, the company that made Hula-Hoops, started selling plastic Frisbees, and the rest is history. Now there are dozens of different types, from glow-in-the-dark Frisbees to discs that are specially designed for disc golf.

Another plastic toy was born from a happy accident. In the early years of World War II, an American scientist was working hard to develop a synthetic rubber for military truck tires. One experiment created a rubberlike substance with special qualities—it could be stretched to incredible lengths without breaking, and it was sticky but did not stay stuck to anything. The military had no interest, and there did not seem to be any practical use for this strange stuff. But when an enterprising toy seller decided to put it into plastic egg-shaped containers and call it Silly Putty, this wacky substance became a popular toy for all ages. The beginning of the plastic age was very exciting! But as plastic production increased, the problems with this material started to emerge.

CHAPTER TWO

Plastic Forever

Does your family have a compost bin? It's fun to watch food scraps and garden waste turn into soil.
HOPSALKA/GETTY IMAGES

Plastic is durable, which means that it lasts for an extremely long time. That's a good thing if you are using plastic to build a bridge or manufacture a bicycle helmet. But the fact that plastic does not break down completely causes a lot of problems for the natural world.

THE BIG PROBLEM

All the plastic that has ever been manufactured is still part of our world today. Birds flying along the coast today can get caught in plastic rings that were tossed out decades ago. In the natural world, there is no waste. Thanks to a process called ***biodegradation***, plants and animals that have reached the end of their lives can be turned into building blocks for creating new life. But plastic does not biodegrade. Discarded plastic disintegrates into smaller pieces, but it never completely breaks down.

Large pieces of plastic break down into smaller and smaller pieces.
WESTEND61/GETTY IMAGES

TEENY PROBLEMS

Plastic pollution is a serious problem. And microplastics—plastic particles that are smaller than a grain of rice—are an especially tricky problem. There are two kinds of microplastics. One kind is designed to be small for a specific reason. For instance, some cosmetic manufacturers add plastic particles to face scrubs because these tiny particles can help get skin extra clean. Some countries, including Canada, have banned the production and sale of personal care products containing microplastics, but there is no international ban.

The other kind of microplastics are plastic objects—everything from forks to visors—that have been broken down by wind, sun and ocean currents into smaller and smaller pieces. Some pieces are so tiny that it is difficult to see them with a microscope! Microplastics are found around the world. They are present everywhere, from tropical rainforests to the Arctic Ocean. As a result, most living creatures, including humans, consume some microplastics every day. Scientists are still investigating how microplastics affect our bodies.

KYTAN/SHUTTERSTOCK.COM

More than 10,000 additives and other chemicals are used in plastic production.

LAURENT DIONNE

My Favorite Fleece

My son Hugh loves his blue fleece. He wears it almost every day in the winter. It is the perfect thing to wear to walk the dog. And it is the perfect thing to wear while skiing and snowshoeing. Hugh also wears his fleece for walking along the beach on summer evenings and sitting around a campfire on chilly fall evenings. Hugh wears his fleece all year long! So he was pretty sad when he heard that most fleece jackets shed a lot of microfibers. Fortunately, there are many ways to reduce microfiber shedding. Now Hugh always washes his fleece in cold water, in a front-loading washing machine, and he washes it as infrequently as possible. Most important, Hugh sets the washing machine on the gentle cycle, which can reduce microfiber shedding by 70 percent.

Each North American household releases approximately 533 million microfibers into wastewater every year.

OUR CLOTHES SHED MICROPLASTICS

Microfibers are tiny, thread-like particles that come off our clothes when we wash, dry and wear them. Natural microfibers may biodegrade, but microfibers from synthetic materials such as nylon and polyester are microplastics, so they do not biodegrade.

Modern water filtration plants are able to remove most of these synthetic microfibers from ***wastewater***, but they cannot remove all of them. Fortunately, an organization in Vancouver, British Columbia, called Ocean Wise is working hard to find ways to decrease the amount of microfibers that enter our waterways via wastewater. Ocean Wise scientists have conducted experiments with 38 different kinds of fabric at their industrial washing-machine test center. They have found that microfibers are more likely to come off some synthetic fabrics than others.

The way you wash your clothes matters! We can all help lower microfiber levels in waterways.

MARTINEDOUCET/GETTY IMAGES

This scientific team also discovered that the rate of microfiber shedding is affected by the type of synthetic material used to make fabrics and also by how the fabrics are constructed. The highest-shedding fabrics lose over 800 times more fibers than the lowest-shedding ones. Polyester fleece, which is made from short filaments of shredded plastic, sheds the most.

Now scientists, clothing manufacturers, washing-machine manufacturers and government officials are working together to learn from these experiments and design products and processes that will help lower the level of microfiber release. It is impossible to remove all the microfibers that are already in the ocean. But it is possible to prevent more microfibers from entering the ocean.

Depending on where they live, people eat and drink anywhere from dozens to more than 100,000 microplastics each day.

OLENA SAKHNENKO/GETTY IMAGES

PLASTIC IN WATER

How does plastic end up in the water? Well, there are many ways. Microplastics in cleaning products can get flushed down the drain and out into the world's waterways. If a ship transporting nurdles or plastic toys has an accident, millions of pieces of plastic can fall overboard into the ocean. Also, some plastic in the ocean comes from abandoned nylon fishing nets. But most of the plastic that is in the ocean actually starts off as land-based waste. Nobody intentionally tosses plastic into the ocean. But tons of it end up there every year because plastic waste is not managed as well as it should be.

Plastic waste washes up on beautiful beaches all over the world—like this one in Greece.
NICK BRUNDLE PHOTOGRAPHY/GETTY IMAGES

A team of Chinese researchers has developed a tiny self-propelled robotic fish that can remove microplastics from the surface of the water. Maybe one day this "fish" will be able to dive under the water.

And plastic is very good at traveling. Imagine for a moment that you are drinking a nice cold soda on a hot day. Then you toss the cup and the straw into a recycling bin. Later on a gust of wind carries the straw into the street. When it rains, the straw goes down a sewer drain. The sewer empties into a river, and the river empties into the ocean. When plastic is tossed "away," it does not disappear. It just goes into a different environment.

TROUBLE FOR OCEAN CREATURES

When plastic gets into the ocean, it can cause a lot of problems for fish, turtles, seabirds and other living creatures. Some creatures get tangled up in plastic debris, such as fishing gear or the plastic rings used on beer and soda cans. Also, some of these creatures accidentally eat plastic because they think it's food. For instance, leatherback turtles love eating jellyfish. Sometimes these turtles eat floating plastic bags by mistake, because they look just like jellyfish. Whales and seabirds like to eat herring eggs. Unfortunately, some microplastic particles look just like herring eggs.

Sea turtles can mistakenly eat plastic bags if they look like jellyfish.

(LEFT) _548901005677/GETTY IMAGES; (RIGHT) AI ANGEL GENTEL/GETTY IMAGES

Seabird chicks that consume a lot of plastic do not develop normally.

KEVIN SCHAFER/GETTY IMAGES

When fish and birds eat plastic instead of their usual food, they stop looking for their usual food because they feel full. Then they can get sick because they are not consuming the nutrients they need to live. Baby birds that are accidentally fed a lot of plastic debris by their parents do not develop properly.

And microplastics are double trouble because lots of dangerous substances, such as disease-causing microbes, ***PCBs*** and the insecticide DDT, "stick" to these teeny particles of plastic. Both PCBs and DDT were banned in Canada and the United States a long time ago, but they are still found in ocean water.

Burning plastic smells bad and fills the air with poisonous chemicals—try to stay far away.
ULADZIMIR CYARGEENKA/GETTY IMAGES

Ninety percent of hazardous emissions from plastic production are in 18 American communities. Most of the people who live in these communities are racialized. This is an example of *environmental racism*.

PLASTIC IN THE AIR

Does plastic affect the air we breathe too? Absolutely! Believe it or not, the problem begins even before plastic is produced, because drilling for the oil and gas used to make plastic causes the release of a lot of toxic chemicals, like benzene and carbon monoxide. And the manufacturing of plastic releases even more hazardous emissions. Also, about 40 percent of the world's garbage—and that includes an increasing amount of plastic—is burned. This is bad news for all creatures that breathe, because burning plastic releases many toxic chemicals into the air.

A lot of medical waste, including used surgical equipment and plastic tubes that were in contact with sick people, is also burned. Fortunately, incineration kills the microbes that cause disease, so they cannot make other people sick. On the other hand, medical waste typically contains a lot of PVC plastic, and burning this type of plastic releases harmful ***dioxins*** into the air.

Finally, microplastics are also present in the air we breathe every day. How does that happen? Well, tires are partly made from plastic. So as vehicles travel along roads and highways and bits of the tires rub off, some tiny pieces of plastic are released. Wind blows the microplastics off the road and up into the air.

PLASTIC AND YOUR BODY

The plastics industry adds thousands of different additives to resins in order to make different kinds of plastic. Some additives make plastic colorful, some additives make plastic soft and squeezable, some make it strong and rigid, and some make it water-repellent. Other additives prevent plastic from breaking down in sunlight or catching fire.

Unfortunately, these additives sometimes leak out of the plastic. Scientists do not know exactly how all these additives affect our bodies. But they do know that a lot of additives disrupt ***hormone messaging***. Sometimes these plastic additives are so similar to hormones that the body becomes confused, and important hormonal messages that are required for normal growth and development are not properly communicated. When you buy a packaged food such as pizza, there is a label listing all the ingredients in the pizza. But right now there is no way for consumers to find out exactly what additives (or ingredients) are in the plastics they use.

North American scientists, governments and businesses are working hard to figure out how to deal with the problems that plastics cause. Our problems are not unique. Every country in the world has plastic problems.

GH DURNFORD-DIONNE

PLASTIC PLANET

Fizzy Water

Our family loves fizzy water, also called carbonated water. One of the best presents we ever received is a device that lets us make our own fizzy water at home. My husband makes sure that we always have some ready to go. Usually we just drink it straight. Sometimes we add a little lemon juice to the water or maybe a little blueberry juice. We never buy plastic beverage bottles from the store, so we never need to worry about where those empty plastic bottles will end up.

CHAPTER THREE

Global Problems Need Global Solutions

Every country is dealing with some form of plastic pollution, from constant plastic litter on the beach to poor air quality due to plastic incineration.

Every year the world produces 450 million tons (408 million metric tons) of plastic waste. About half of it is single-use waste.

WHO TAKES CARE OF THE OCEAN?

What about places that don't belong to any country—like the Great Pacific Garbage Patch (GPGP), which is halfway between California and Hawaii? Tons of different-sized plastic pieces have collected in this area because they are caught in a ***gyre.*** Contrary to popular belief, the GPGP is not a big island of garbage. It is more like a "soup" that is more than 600,000 square miles (1.6 million square kilometers) wide. There are also four other less-famous plastic "soups" in the world's oceans.

A lot of plastic waste washes up on beaches.
ANTONIO HUGO PHOTO/GETTY IMAGES

Fortunately, several international organizations, made up of people from around the world, are tackling the complex issue of plastic pollution in the ocean. The 5 Gyres Institute, for instance, was founded to answer such questions as how much plastic pollution is in the ocean, what impact plastic has on people and the planet and, of course, the biggest question of all: what can humanity do about this global crisis?

Unfortunately, it is impossible to remove all plastic pollution from the ocean because so much of the plastic waste is already below the surface. Over time plastic objects break up into smaller and smaller pieces. These microplastics start to sink, like falling snow, to the bottom of the ocean. Once plastic is on the ocean floor, it is there to stay. There is not yet an obvious way to remove it.

Most of the floating plastic in the GPGP comes from nets, ropes, buckets, floats and other plastic products used in commercial fishing activities.

THE OCEAN CLEANUP

Some organizations, such as The Ocean Cleanup (OC), are doing what they can to remove plastic that is at or near the ocean surface. In 2011 Dutch teenager Boyan Slat went on a diving holiday to Greece. He was shocked when he saw more plastic than fish! So once back at home, Slat and a fellow classmate did a science project about plastic marine pollution to raise awareness of this issue. When he was at university, Slat was still so haunted by this problem that he founded OC, an organization dedicated to removing plastic from the ocean.

There is 10,000 times more microplastic on the bottom of the ocean than there is in contaminated surface water.

In 2021, after years of experimentation, OC announced that it finally had a system that worked. This system is composed of two large ships connected by a long, flexible V-shaped floating barrier that collects and concentrates the plastic waste. OC has successfully removed about 220 tons (200 metric tons) of plastic waste from the ocean. But there is a long way to go! There are approximately 165 million tons (150 million metric tons) of plastic pollution in the ocean. We really need to focus on stopping the flow of plastic into the ocean in the first place.

The Ocean Cleanup's System 002 is helping remove plastic from the Pacific Ocean.
THE OCEAN CLEANUP

HEADING DOWN THE RIVER

Researchers have determined that 80 percent of all plastic waste is transported to the ocean via 1,000 of the world's rivers, especially urban rivers. Different technology has been deployed around the globe to try to prevent this plastic waste from reaching the ocean. One innovative system, used in Amsterdam, employs a stream of bubbles to force plastic waste in rivers and canals to the surface so that it can be easily removed. It does not disrupt wildlife or boat traffic. Another system involves floating barriers that funnel plastic waste toward a solar-powered conveyor belt system, which automatically uploads it. An artificial intelligence system that is still in development will feature an ***autonomous*** vessel that can detect and remove plastic waste as it moves around a harbor.

In Amsterdam, a curtain of air bubbles forces plastic waste in the water to the surface, making it easier to remove the waste.

THE GREAT BUBBLE BARRIER

THE LAST STEP

There are many effective programs to collect plastic waste from waterways and the ocean. This is wonderful news! But true success means making sure that this collected waste is recycled responsibly so that it doesn't just end up back where it began.

Do you know where to put your used or unwanted plastic? Is it recyclable or is it garbage?

AZMANL/GETTY IMAGES

Properly dispose of your used face mask to help prevent the spread of sickness.

GOADS AGENCY/GETTY IMAGES

PANDEMIC PLASTIC

When you think of COVID-19, you probably think about a sickness that made people cough and feel feverish, right? So what does COVID-19 have to do with plastic? During the pandemic, citizens everywhere were asked to wear face masks. And healthcare workers were provided with disposable protective gear. These policies helped protect a lot of people from getting sick with COVID-19, but unfortunately they also made the world's plastic-pollution problem much worse. During the lockdown, 1.8 million tons (1.6 million metric tons) of plastic waste per day—from disposable gloves, face masks, face shields, syringes and protective medical suits to shoe covers and medical test kits—were added to the world's already-severe plastic overload.

None of these items are recyclable. Some of them are in landfills, some have been incinerated and some are traveling around in the natural environment. Apart from medical waste, the COVID-19 pandemic led to an increase in other kinds of plastic pollution too. For instance, during the most acute phases of the pandemic, restaurants were only permitted to sell takeout food. So millions of meals that might normally have been eaten off washable plates with metal cutlery in a restaurant were placed in disposable plastic containers and packaged with disposable plastic cutlery and straws. During the pandemic, online food-delivery services increased dramatically.

Avignon

Single-use plastics, such as plastic cutlery, straws and food and drink containers, are banned in Europe. So European businesses have had to figure out lots of innovative ways to manage without disposable plastic. In Avignon, in southern France, I discovered Vivotto, a small business that sold prêt-à-manger (that's French for "ready to eat") meals. They had all kinds of interesting lunch and dinner options, such as risotto Calabria, lasagne alla Bolognese and lentil salad. All the meals are packaged in beautiful glass containers with glass lids. First, customers select a meal, and then they decide whether they want to eat at the restaurant or buy the meal for takeout and heat it up at home. For takeout, customers are asked to pay a small deposit for the container. This deposit is refunded once the container is returned. Vivotto does not generate any plastic waste. And no one has to worry about plastic additives getting into their food. What a delicious solution!

LAURENT DIONNE

Some plastic waste travels around the world.
(MAIN) BUGTO/GETTY IMAGES; (INSET) MIODRAG IGNJATOVIC/GETTY IMAGES

PLASTIC ON THE MOVE

Plastic waste moves around the globe in many different ways. Some plastic travels via wind and ocean currents. And some of it is intentionally shipped from wealthy countries to developing countries. Under international law, each country should take care of its own garbage, close to where the garbage was produced. But the reality is that it is often cheaper for companies in wealthy countries to ship plastic waste to other countries than to process it at home.

Until recently China received regular shipments of plastic waste from North America. Chinese businesses eagerly bought this used plastic and recycled it into new products in order to meet global market demand. For instance, used plastic water bottles from North America were transformed into polyester fiber for making fabric. Unfortunately, many of these shipments

The worst maritime disaster in Sri Lanka, in 2021, was caused by plastic. After a container ship caught fire and sank, 87 shipping containers full of nurdles were accidentally released into the ocean.

In developing countries, 20 million people rely on waste picking, sorting and recycling for their livelihoods.

contained both the plastic waste that had been purchased by Chinese companies and other undesirable plastic. In 2018 China became fed up with this situation and shut its door on foreign waste.

Then wealthy countries, including Canada, began sending their unwanted plastic to other Asian countries, such as Malaysia, the Philippines and India. You might wonder how countries can just send their waste to another country. One explanation is incorrectly labeled shipping containers. Sometimes unwanted plastic is intentionally hidden by combining it with another material that the developing country is waiting to receive, such as mixed paper. After the paper mill removes the paper from the shipment, no one really keeps track of what happens to the plastic waste.

Waste pickers look through garbage dumps for items that they can reuse or resell.

RICCARDO MAYER/SHUTTERSTOCK.COM

NEW RULES

Most developing countries are still trying to contain the plastic waste produced within their own borders, so it is not surprising that they can't manage waste arriving from other countries. Much of the unwanted plastic that arrives in developing countries is burned as fuel by local people because it is so much cheaper than firewood and other available fuel options. As you read in chapter 2, it is very unhealthy to breathe in fumes from burning plastic.

In 2019 representatives from most of the world's countries signed an agreement to better manage international transportation of plastic waste. Businesses can continue to import and export post-consumer plastic waste, like other goods. But now there are conditions. The plastic waste must be free of contamination, it must not be hazardous, and it must be destined for recycling in an environmentally sound manner.

Recycling plants sort hundreds of different kinds of plastic.

MASSIMO BORCHI/ATLANTIDE PHOTOTRAVEL/GETTY IMAGES

HADYNYAH/GETTY IMAGES

India

After university I traveled around India by train. The trains did not always leave and arrive on schedule. But one thing I loved about train travel was that whenever the train stopped at a station, I could buy a freshly made cup of chai (a sweet, milky tea) from a vendor on the train platform. I did not even need to get off the train. Then, after I drank my chai, I simply tossed the biodegradable clay cup out the window.

Not surprisingly, many chai vendors began to use plastic cups instead of clay cups, because plastic is really cheap. But as passengers began to toss those cups out of train windows, plastic litter began to pile up along the railway lines. Apparently, clay cups are making a comeback at Indian railway stations now. This makes me really happy, because clay cups are much more eco-friendly than plastic—plus, the chai tastes so much better from a clay cup!

The plastics industry depends on the oil and gas industry for raw materials.
DAN_PRAT/GETTY IMAGES

PLASTIC AND THE CLIMATE

Plastic pollution is the second most serious environmental problem in the world. But did you know that plastic also plays an important role in climate change—the world's most serious environmental issue? First the good news. In some instances, plastic can help lower ***greenhouse gas emissions*** from vehicles. Most cars, planes and boats are powered by fossil fuels. Heavier vehicles use more fuel than light vehicles to go the same distance. So if some vehicle parts, such as hoods and roofs, are made out of reinforced plastic instead of metal, the vehicle is lighter and generates fewer greenhouse gases per mile.

Unfortunately, most of the news is bad news, because greenhouse gases are emitted at every single stage of plastic's life cycle. If plastic were a country, it would be the fifth-largest emitter. In the first chapter we looked at how plastic is made, but what about the emissions that are created as it's being produced?

Emissions are released:

- when land is ***fracked***
- when the fracked gases are captured and shipped to a facility that processes them into other gases, such as ethane
- at "cracker" plants, where ethane gas is superheated and cracked into new chemicals, such as ethylene
- as ethylene is shipped to plastic-production factories in the United States, Europe and Asia to make plastic bags
- during the production of plastic bags
- when discarded plastic grocery bags are exposed to sunlight

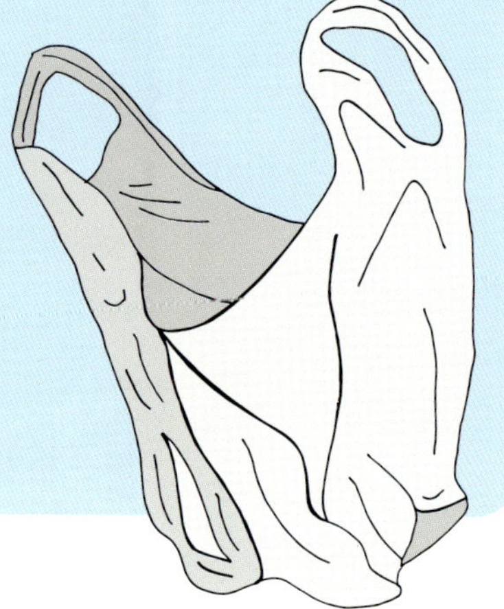

The United Nations is helping resolve our international plastic problem.

ALXPIN/GETTY IMAGES

WORKING TOGETHER

Many cities and countries around the world have passed laws to try to manage plastic pollution. But plastic is always "on the move." It is increasingly clear that managing plastic pollution requires international ***collaboration***. At a United Nations meeting in Nairobi, Kenya, representatives from 175 countries decided to work together on issues associated with plastic. These policymakers have agreed to study every step of plastic's life cycle, from production to disposal. And they will look at a wide range of possible solutions. For instance, producing more plastic products that can be reused or recycled could help lower the level of plastic waste in natural environments.

The policymakers have committed to review the latest scientific research regarding plastic production, recycling and disposal, as well as plastic alternatives. But they will also listen to local knowledge keepers and the perspective of plastic-waste pickers who depend on income they get from plastic collection.

They will consider how countries can best work together to share scientific and technical information. Then the policymakers will draw up a legally binding document to ensure that countries that officially approve the final document are obliged to follow its recommendations. This is crucial. If a treaty is not legally binding, participating countries can choose to disregard the report recommendations.

So now you know a lot about why we need to change our relationship with plastic. Are you ready to hear about some of the really neat ways we can do that?

This art installation by international artist and activist Benjamin Von Wong was displayed at the United Nations headquarters in Nairobi, Kenya.

BENJAMIN VON WONG, *GIANT PLASTIC TAP*, VONWONG.COM

CHAPTER FOUR

Beyond Plastic

The virtual-reality project Plastisapiens *allows you to enter a world in which organic beings and plastic have become one.*
JURRE ROMPA

Plastic is hard to replace. It's lightweight, flexible and durable—and it's cheap! But it is clear that we humans need to break away from our plastic habits to avoid more environmental problems. There are all kinds of potential solutions, such as reducing plastic production, developing alternatives to plastic and improving the management of plastic waste. There is no perfect solution to the plastic crisis, however. We will need to work toward all possible solutions at the same time.

REPLACE

Could we just start making plastic from other sources, such as corn, instead of petrochemicals? Would these bio-based plastic objects biodegrade and become part of the natural environment like decomposing trees? Unfortunately, it is a bit more complicated than that. The first issue is vocabulary.

Compostable plastic sounds good, but is it truly compostable?

(LEFT) MIKE DOTTA/SHUTTERSTOCK.COM;
(RIGHT) PETER IS SHAW 1991/SHUTTERSTOCK.COM

The term *bio-based plastic* is confusing. Believe it or not, there are no official international definitions for this term. Manufacturers can sell "bio-based" plastic that contains all kinds of other stuff, like fossil fuels and toxic additives. Contrary to popular belief, bio-based plastic is not necessarily better for the environment.

What about "compostable" plastic? This type of plastic can completely biodegrade under specific conditions. If it is carefully collected, sorted and sent to an appropriate industrial composting facility, that's super! But what happens if you live in an area that doesn't have such a facility? Unfortunately, the "compostable" plastic will probably be sent to landfill.

Consumer behavior—why we buy the things we do—is also an important part of this issue. Creating alternatives to conventional plastic is an important step. But people who use bio-based plastic products need to understand what to do with them to avoid creating a whole new set of problems. For instance, when people put products made of ***PLA***, a bio-based plastic that looks like conventional plastic, into their recycling boxes, they can (accidentally!) disrupt conventional plastic recycling.

Researchers are developing edible, tasteless and invisible plant-based coatings to keep fruits and vegetables fresh. These coatings aim to keep moisture in and oxygen out, so that produce does not need to be wrapped in plastic bags.

HUGH DURNFORD-DIONNE

Beeswax Wrapping

In my daughter Charlotte's neighborhood, you are not allowed to put plastic film in the recycling box. Charlotte did not want to toss plastic film into the garbage, so she decided to make her own food wrapping. First she grates beeswax with a cheese grater (it looks a bit like grated parmesan). Then she sprinkles the beeswax onto squares of 100 percent cotton cloth. Next Charlotte sprinkles a few drops of jojoba oil over the beeswax. The jojoba is not essential, but it makes the coated squares extra sticky, which makes them easy to use. Finally Charlotte places the fabric squares between two layers of parchment paper and starts ironing. Ta-da! In a few moments her new food wrapping is ready for use.

Children help catch invasive green crabs as part of a Parks Canada citizen science program in Nova Scotia.

(MAIN) PARKS CANADA; (INSET) HHELENE/GETTY IMAGES

WASTE TO BIOPLASTIC

European green crabs are one of the world's most aggressive ***invasive species***. And these little monsters have already caused a lot of damage to the marine ecosystem of southwest Nova Scotia. Fortunately, McGill University chemistry professor Audrey Moores has found a way to turn the problematic crabs into biopolymers, which can be used for making bioplastic. She has solved two problems at once! Using ***green chemistry***, Moores has developed a sustainable way to extract ***chitin*** from the crabs' shells. And chitin, which can't dissolve in water, is a great candidate for making bioplastic. Every year several million tons of ***crustacean*** waste is produced around the globe. One day plastic made from crustacean waste may replace some types of conventional plastic!

Luna Yu, in Toronto, has another great idea. When Yu was a child, her grandparents taught her that it was very important not to waste food. Now Yu is an adult, and she runs Genecis Bioindustries, a company that helps prevent food waste. Scientists at Genecis have developed a process that uses special bacteria to turn household food scraps into ***PHA***, another biopolymer that can be used to make bioplastic. Making PHA from food waste is much cheaper than other ways of making it, so the process has a lot of potential.

RECYCLING DAY

Most North American families take recycling very seriously. After all, it feels good to put plastic containers into the recycling box and not the garbage bin. But is the plastic that we put into the recycling box actually recycled? That is a very big question. First of all, it depends on where you live. If you live in British Columbia, then you can rest assured that all your plastic packaging waste is responsibly managed—meaning a high percentage of it is recycled. In the United States, California leads the way in strategies to reduce plastic pollution. Unfortunately, many North American municipalities are so cash-strapped that a lot of potentially recyclable material is sent to landfills.

Oregon implemented the first bottle-deposit-and-return system in the United States, in 1972.

Read signs carefully so that you put your waste in the right container.

MASKOT/GETTY IMAGES

At a high-tech recycling facility in southern France, a variety of sensors detect specific types of plastic and then direct robotic arms to retrieve selected items.
WASTE ROBOTICS

BETTER SORTING

One reason recycling plastic is so complicated is that there are so many different kinds of plastic waste. Also, it is very difficult for manual sorters at recycling plants to watch for and sort recyclable items quickly. New technology involving robotics and artificial intelligence is helping make plastic waste sorting more efficient. Not only are robotic arms faster than human sorters, but robotic systems can be trained to "see" things that humans cannot.

For instance, at a sophisticated recycling center in France, a special camera uses laser light to "see" the exact composition of plastic waste on the conveyor belt. Then robots place all the plastic made from the same material in the same bin. Bins with the same kinds of used plastic are worth more than bins of mixed plastic. Believe it or not, these robots can also learn new concepts through experience (the way you do!), making them better at their jobs. And they can share this new information with other robots.

Another new approach to improve plastic waste sorting is identification technology. The PRISM system, for instance, adds invisible markers to the labels of specific plastic containers. Under ultraviolet light, equipment can "see" the special labels easily, and the marked containers can be separated out from the rest of the plastic waste.

In Japan all PET bottles are clear (not colored) so it's much easier and faster to process them at the recycling plant. This is one reason why Japan has an extremely high recycling rate for PET bottles.

MECHANICAL RECYCLING

Mechanical recycling is not new, but it is becoming more common. It involves transforming plastic waste made from a specific type of resin into pellets that can be used to create all kinds of new plastic products, such as plastic bottles, garbage bags, paint trays, residential siding and plastic shelving. Plastic waste has value if there is a potential end market, and there are manufacturers who want to buy a specific type of recycled plastic pellets to make new products.

Recycled pellets made from such plastics as ***PET***, HDPE and polypropylene have lots of end markets. Technology exists to create pellets from other types of plastic waste too, such as plastic film. But plastic recyclers are limited by access to good sources of these used plastics (due to collection and sorting issues), and there are not enough buyers for the recycled pellets.

Another important challenge for plastic recyclers is that it is often much cheaper for plastic-product manufacturers to make their products with new plastic pellets, not recycled ones. This situation will likely change once these manufacturers are obliged by law to use a specific amount of recycled plastic. Many countries have already set ambitious goals to increase the percentage of recycled content in new plastic products. By 2030 in Canada, all plastic packaging will be required to contain at least 50 percent recycled content.

This NoNetz swim top is made from fishing net and other nylon waste. Your fashion choices can help keep plastic out of the ocean.

NONETZ

In 1988 the Society of the Plastics Industry (now known as the Plastics Industry Association) introduced a system of symbols to help manufacturers indicate the kind of plastic used. These symbols are not a guarantee of recycling, however. Many consumers wrongly assume that plastic items labeled with this symbol are automatically recycled.

IVAN YAROVYI/GETTY IMAGES

CHEMICAL RECYCLING

Chemical recycling uses high heat in an oxygen-free setting to melt and ***depolymerize*** some kinds of plastic waste. One advantage of chemical recycling is that it can be used to process a blend of different plastic resins at the same time. The downside is that this type of recycling can create hazardous byproducts and it is much more expensive than mechanical recycling. Chemical recycling may play a role in reducing plastic pollution, but for now, it is a very minor role.

It's fun to drink from a juice box! Too bad that most juice boxes are not recyclable.
JUPITERIMAGES/GETTY IMAGES

GAME CHANGER

As we've discovered, less than 9 percent of plastic waste in North America is recycled. The main explanation for this shocking situation is that most of the plastic containers we use every day were never designed to be recycled. It's time to rethink the whole system! What if the companies that produce goods started to play a bigger role in waste management? This concept, called ***extended producer responsibility*** (EPR), is starting to gain traction.

Have you ever helped your parents take bottles back to the store? Most North American supermarkets participate in a bottle-deposit-and-return system. Consumers pay a small deposit when they purchase a bottle and get the deposit back when the bottle is returned. This system helps ensure that bottles are recycled and do not end up in the landfill. Now imagine if there were a system to manage all kinds of other containers. There is!

What do you do with plastic bottles in your neighborhood?
ANDREW FOX/GETTY IMAGES

EUROPEAN IDEAS

Germany is an EPR pioneer. More than three decades ago, as this country's landfills were close to overflowing, Germany insisted that manufacturers take responsibility for the entire life cycle of the goods they put on the market, from production to disposal. How does EPR work? In a nutshell, product manufacturers pay fees, based on the quantity and weight of products sold, to special organizations that manage the collection and sorting of packaging waste. Then these organizations sell some of the recycled material to other companies. EPR works because it motivates manufacturers to make their packages easier to recycle. Thanks to strict waste-management legislation and public participation, Germany now boasts one of the highest recycling rates in Europe.

EPR programs have been adopted all over Europe. In North America, some provinces and states are starting to adopt this concept too. Recycle BC is a very successful EPR organization that manages recycling in British Columbia. This nonprofit organization, financed by local producers and retailers, manages the collection and recycling of all paper and packaging in the province. Recycle BC is also helping make packaging more recyclable, so that more items are recycled and fewer are sent to landfills. One approach is to encourage producers to follow new design guidelines, such as minimizing packaging, eliminating hard-to-recycle items, such as juice boxes, and ensuring that container labels are easy to remove.

In Germany there are reverse vending machines in supermarkets. This technology makes it even easier for people to recycle plastic and glass bottles.

ELVA ETIENNE/GETTY IMAGES

REDUCE

More-efficient plastic recycling, bio-based plastic and EPR are all great ideas, but these approaches are not enough. Less plastic production, especially of single-use products, needs to be part of the equation. This will not be easy! One approach is to remember how people managed before plastic existed.

At farmers' markets, fresh fruits and vegetables are not wrapped in plastic.

STEPHEN SIMPSON/GETTY IMAGES

For instance, you can prioritize buying clothing made from cotton, linen and wool instead of synthetic fabrics. Another approach is to prioritize reusable items. You probably already know about reusable water bottles and reusable shopping bags. As single-use plastic bans come into effect across North America, lots of new reusable products and programs are popping up. Restaurants all over North America are starting to offer reusable takeout containers. These reuse programs offer different types of membership plans. And they use different types of containers. Some containers are round and some are rectangular. Some are made from high-grade polypropylene plastic and others are made from stainless steel.

One thing these programs have in common is that they all use digital technology, such as downloadable applications and QR codes, to keep track of the food containers, from restaurant pickup to return. Eventually caterers, institutions, supermarkets and fast-food franchises will likely adopt reusable containers too. At the end of the day, we will all need to develop new habits. When your library books are due to be returned, you probably return them, right? So in the future, when your reusable containers need to be returned, you will probably remember to return them too.

AZMANL/GETTY IMAGES

Refill Store

Refill stores and bulk-food stores make it easy to avoid bringing home lots of plastic packaging. At the refill store near my house, I can buy nonperishable foods like black beans and oatmeal, packaged in uniformly sized glass jars. I pay a deposit for each jar. When I return the empty jars, the deposits are refunded. Also, I can bring my own containers to fill with balsamic vinegar, kombucha, shampoo and all kinds of other liquid products. I like the fact that I can buy the exact amount I want. This little store may not sell everything I need to buy, but I am definitely creating less plastic waste than I was before.

After you return your reusable food container to the collection site, it is disinfected. Then your container can be used by another customer, which reduces waste.

HUGH DURNFORD-DIONNE

WHAT CAN YOU DO?

Plastic is an incredible substance. It can benefit us, yet it can also cause serious problems. Now we must all join forces and work together to improve our relationship with this unique material. There are lots of ways that you can help too.

Don't use single-use plastic cutlery. Bring a reusable set of cutlery with you when you are eating takeout.

Reuse plastic binders for your class notes instead of buying new ones.

Organize a field trip to the local recycling facility.

Keep a refillable water bottle with you so that you are not tempted to buy a plastic water bottle.

Is some of your food wrapped in nonrecyclable packaging? Send it back to the manufacturer and ask for an explanation.

Research some aspect of plastic for your next presentation at school.

Ask your grandparents how they managed before plastic existed. Do they have any good ideas?

Help clean up plastic litter from your schoolyard and neighborhood.

Fill birthday-party loot bags with homemade treats instead of plastic toys.

Encourage your family to look for products made with recycled plastic.

Support restaurants that use reusable takeout containers.

Join a community beach, river or wetland cleanup. On June 8, World Oceans Day, there are events around the world.

ROW 1: RORYGEZ FRESH/GETTY IMAGES, AIRE IMAGES/GETTY IMAGES, ANDRESR/GETTY IMAGES, PETER MULLER/GETTY IMAGES

ROW 2: DIGIPUB/GETTY IMAGES, ARIEL SKELLEY/GETTY IMAGES, TIMOFEY ZADVORNOV/GETTY IMAGES, KLINGSUP/GETTY IMAGES

ROW 3: SOLSTOCK/GETTY IMAGES, TOM WERNER/GETTY IMAGES, YEVGENIIA VRADII/GETTY IMAGES, WESTEND61/GETTY IMAGES

Resources

Print

Beer, Julie. *Kids vs Plastic: Ditch the Straw and Find the Pollution Solution to Bottles, Bags, and Other Single-Use Plastics.* National Geographic Kids, 2020.

Eriksson, Ann. *Dive In! Exploring Our Connection with the Ocean.* Orca Book Publishers, 2018.

Hood, Susan. *The Last Straw: Kids vs Plastics.* HarperCollins, 2021.

Kim, Eun-Ju. *Plastic: Past, Present and Future.* Scribble, 2019.

Mulder, Michelle. *Trash Talk: Moving Toward a Zero-Waste World.* Orca Book Publishers, 2015.

Newman, Patricia. *Plastic, Ahoy: Investigating the Great Pacific Garbage Patch.* Millbrook Press, 2014.

Paul, Miranda. *One Plastic Bag: Isatou Ceesay and the Recycling Women of the Gambia.* Millbrook Press, 2015.

Online

5 Gyres Institute: 5gyres.org

Beyond Plastic: beyondplastics.org

Canada Plastics Pact: plasticspact.ca

David Suzuki Foundation: davidsuzuki.org

Ellen MacArthur Foundation: ellenmacarthurfoundation.org

Greenpeace: greenpeace.org

Kids against Plastic: kidsagainstplastic.co.uk

Ocean Wise: ocean.org

Oceana: oceana.org

Plastic Free July: plasticfreejuly.org

Plastic Pollution Coalition: plasticpollutioncoalition.org

The Ocean Cleanup: theoceancleanup.com

Glossary

autonomous—able to act independently

billiards—a game similar to pool that is played on a special table

biodegradation—the decomposition of natural materials via sunlight, wind, rain and microorganisms into potential building blocks for new life

cellulose—a substance that is present in the cell walls of plants

chitin—a complex sugar in the hard covering of insects and crustaceans

collaboration—the process of working together toward a common goal

crustacean—an invertebrate animal with a hard shell and antennae, such as crab, lobster and shrimp

depolymerize—to break up a polymer into smaller molecules

dioxins—toxic chemicals that can disrupt the immune system and the reproductive system

environmental racism—the disproportionate presence of incinerators, landfills and other forms of hazardous waste in racialized communities

ethane—a type of gas that is derived from natural gas. Ethane is used in the first stage of plastic production.

extended producer responsibility—a system in which the producer of an object takes responsibility for the disposal of that object

fossil fuels—fuels formed in the earth from the decomposition of plants and animals

fracked—injected chemicals into a fissure under pressure in order to extract fossil fuel

green chemistry—the design of chemical processes and products that reduce or eliminate the use or generation of hazardous substances

greenhouse gas emissions—emissions of gases that absorb infrared radiation and trap heat in the atmosphere

gyre—a spiraling ocean current driven by wind

hormone messaging—a chemical messenger system that tells our bodies how to manage growth, reproduction and metabolism

invasive species—a plant or animal species that spreads and causes problems when it is moved (usually by humans) to a new environment

microbes—extremely small organisms that cannot be seen without a microscope, such as bacteria

molecular bonds—connections between molecules

nurdles—small plastic pellets produced by the plastics industry that are designed to be melted down and molded into a wide range of plastic objects

PCBs—polychlorinated biphenyls, toxic substances that were once used in industrial settings, such as insulation to protect electric equipment from high temperatures

PET—polyethylene terephthalate, a type of plastic that is commonly used for beverage containers

petrochemical plants—factories where oil and gas are processed into a variety of chemical products

PHA—polyhydroxyalkanoate, a biopolymer that serves as an energy source for certain types of bacteria

phthalates—common plastic additives that are associated with hormonal disruption

PLA—polylactic acid, a biopolymer present in starch-rich plants, such as corn, sugarcane or potatoes

polymers—large molecules made up of smaller molecules that are chemically linked together

PVC—polyvinyl chloride, a plastic also known as vinyl

resin—a specific type of plastic

wastewater—used water that is flushed away, usually from a home or an industrial building

Index

Page numbers in **bold** *indicate an image caption.*

Acknowledgments

First, I would like to thank my amazing family—my dear husband, Larry, and our children, Hugh and Charlotte—who eagerly listened to endless anecdotes about all things "plastic" and who generously contributed their creative talents to this book. Thanks also to my mother, Nancy, who recycled long before the advent of recycling boxes and sparked my interest in environmental science.

I am extremely grateful to a wide range of experts who helped me better understand the complex role of plastic in our society: Duncan Bury, Sarah Dudas, Dr. Shreyas Patankar, Alexis Goldsmith, Michael Doshi, Martin Vogt, Sabaa Khan, Erica Cirino, Dr. Audrey Moores, Katherine Diamond and Mishel Wong.

Special thanks to Kirstie Hudson, editor extraordinaire, and the wonderful Orca team. It has been a real pleasure to collaborate with you.

Also, I would like to thank librarian Julia Dudley, at the Special Collections Research Center of Syracuse University Libraries, for helping me locate photos about the history of plastic.

And thanks so much to the Refill &co store in Westmount for enabling a photo shoot.

Finally, thanks to librarians Wendy Wayling and Rennie MacLeod for helping me connect with youth consultants. Thanks to all the youth consultants at ECS school in Montreal. And special thanks to youth consultants Elenor Keller, Romane Beauregard-Gagné and Charlie Reuter.

LAURENT DIONNE

A born storyteller, **MEGAN DURNFORD** is a writer, arts journalist and documentary filmmaker. She is the author of two nonfiction books: *René Lévesque: The Fascinating Life of a Separatist Icon* and *Christmas in Quebec: Heartwarming Legends, Tales and Traditions.*

Megan's interest in environmental science stems from her love of the natural world. Her first documentary film, *Just a Lawn*, highlighted Quebec's pioneering ban on cosmetic pesticides and the dark side of "perfect lawns."

Megan lives in Montreal with her family.